This
Coloring Book
Belongs To

_____

Pride And Prejudice

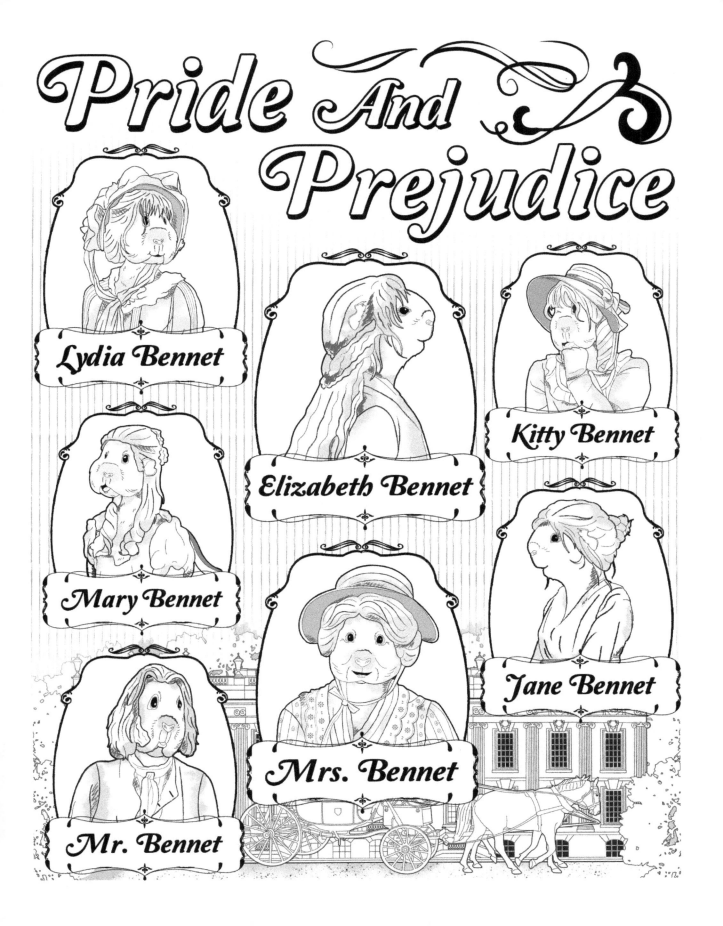

Lydia Bennet

Elizabeth Bennet

Kitty Bennet

Mary Bennet

Jane Bennet

Mr. Bennet

Mrs. Bennet

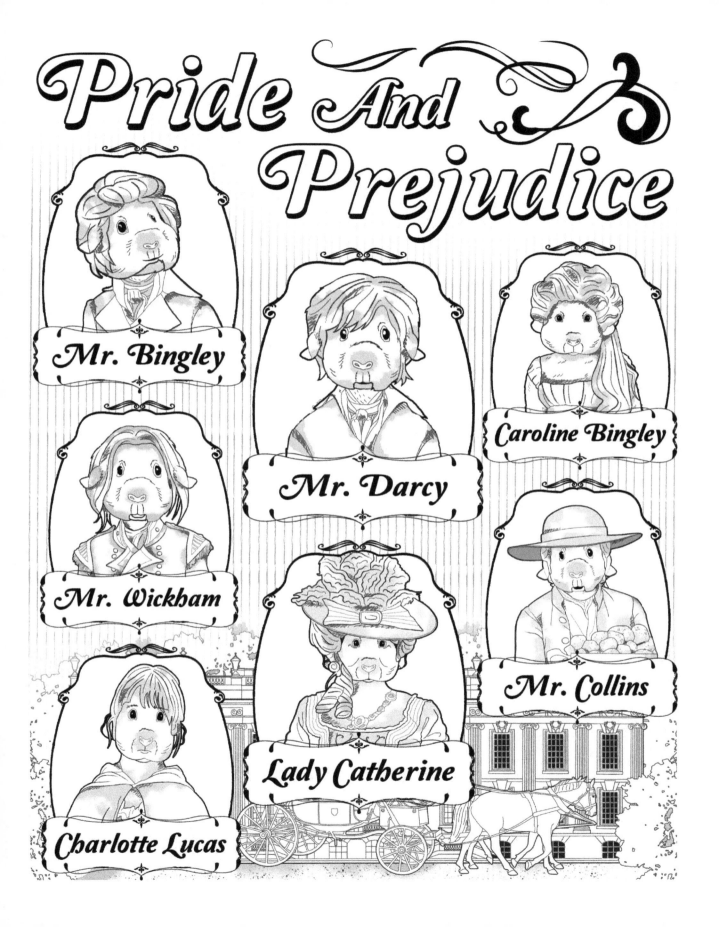

Pride And Prejudice

Mr. Bingley

Mr. Darcy

Caroline Bingley

Mr. Wickham

Mr. Collins

Charlotte Lucas

Lady Catherine

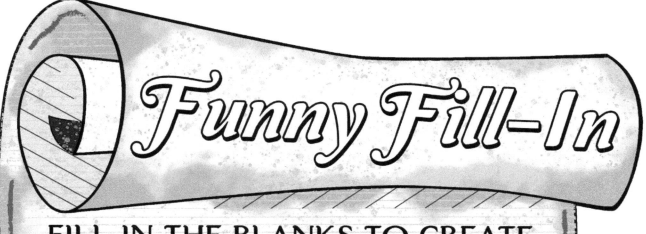

Funny Fill-In

FILL IN THE BLANKS TO CREATE
YOUR OWN SILLY STORY
THEN TURN TO THE NEXT PAGE. >>>

"

_____
(adjective)

_____
(noun (should be a living thing))

"

_____.
(noun)

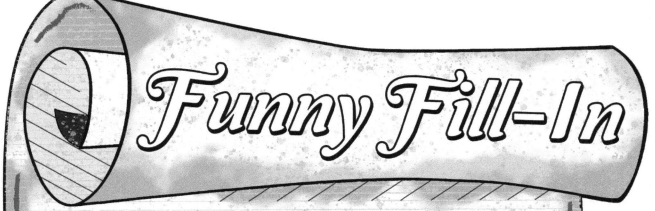

Funny Fill-In

FILL IN THE BLANKS TO CREATE
YOUR OWN SILLY STORY

"*It Is A Truth Universally Acknowledged, That A* _____
(adjective)

_____ *In Possession*
(noun (should be a living thing))

Of A Good Fortune, Must Be In Want Of A _____."
(noun)

Oh! Single, my dear, to be sure!
A single man of large fortune,
four or five thousand a year.
What a fine thing for our girls!

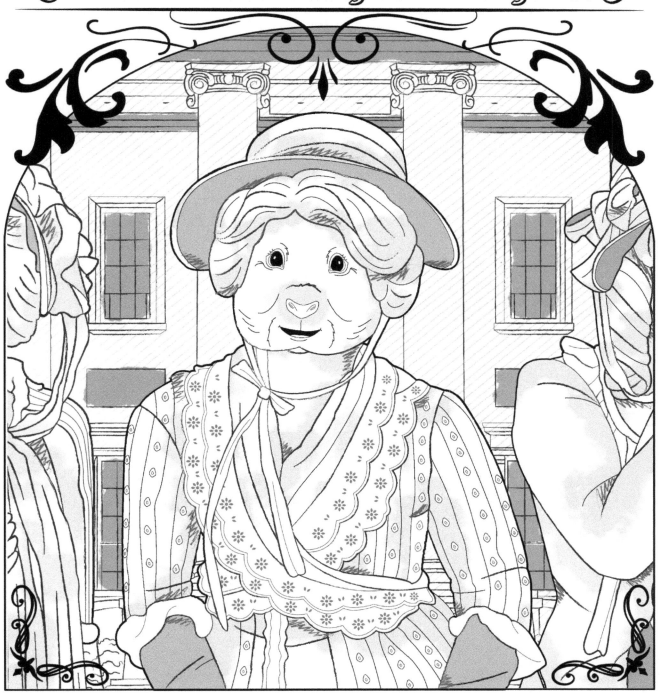

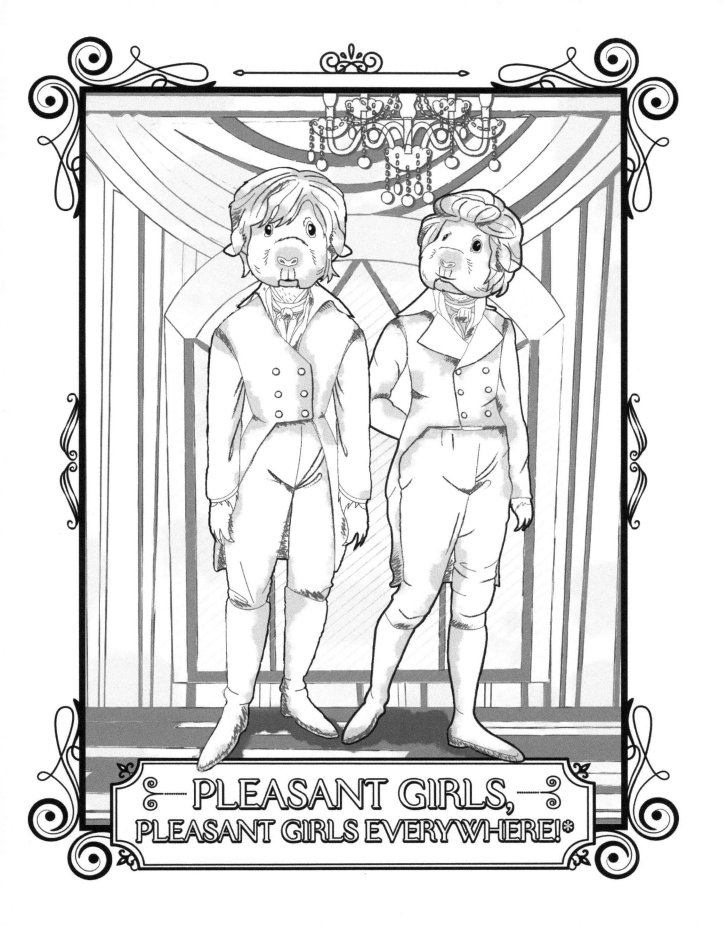

PLEASANT GIRLS,
PLEASANT GIRLS EVERYWHERE!*

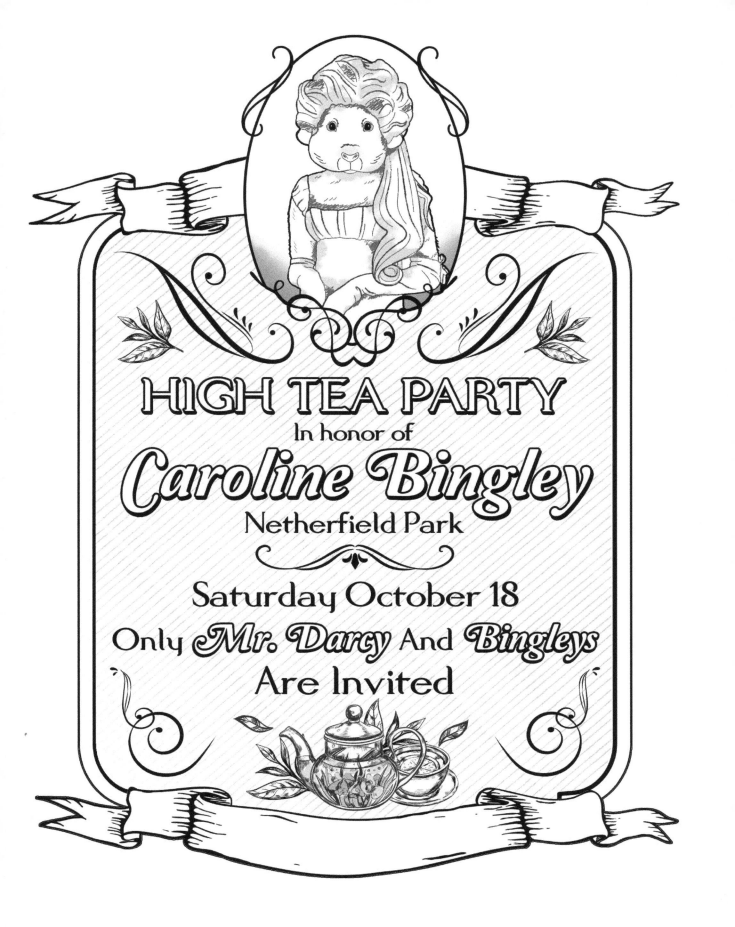

HIGH TEA PARTY

In honor of

Caroline Bingley

Netherfield Park

Saturday October 18

Only *Mr. Darcy* And *Bingleys*

Are Invited

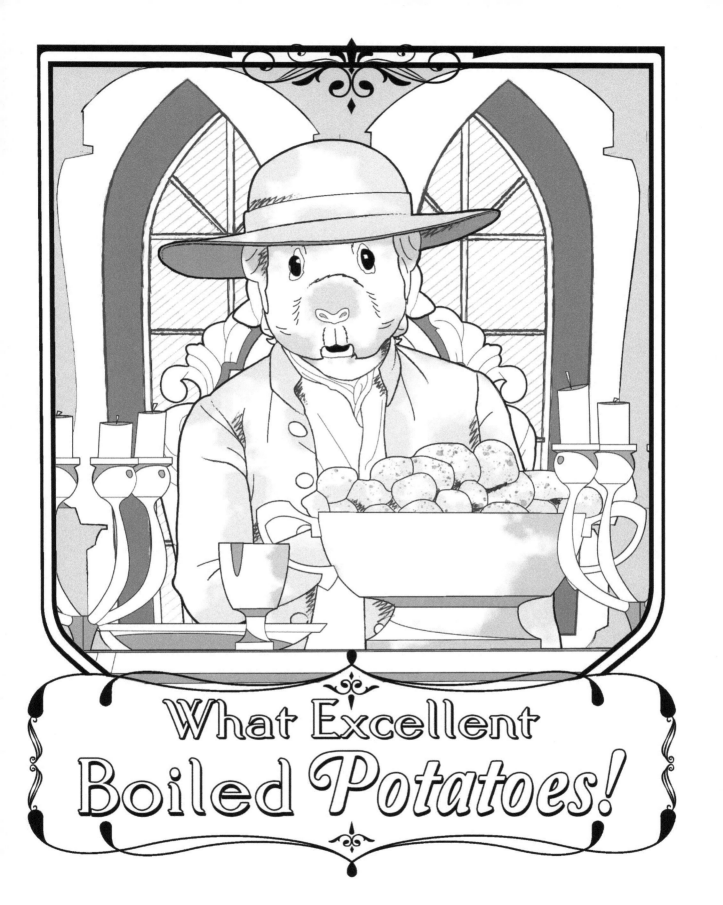

What Excellent Boiled Potatoes!

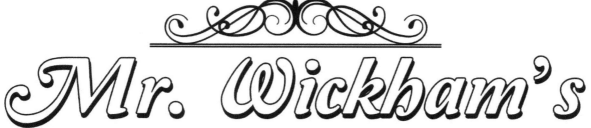

Mr. Wickham's

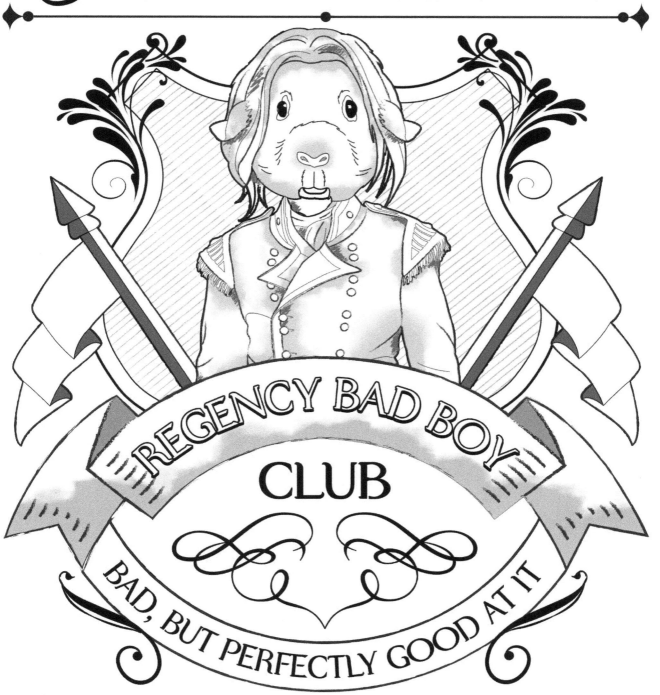

REGENCY BAD BOY

CLUB

BAD, BUT PERFECTLY GOOD AT IT

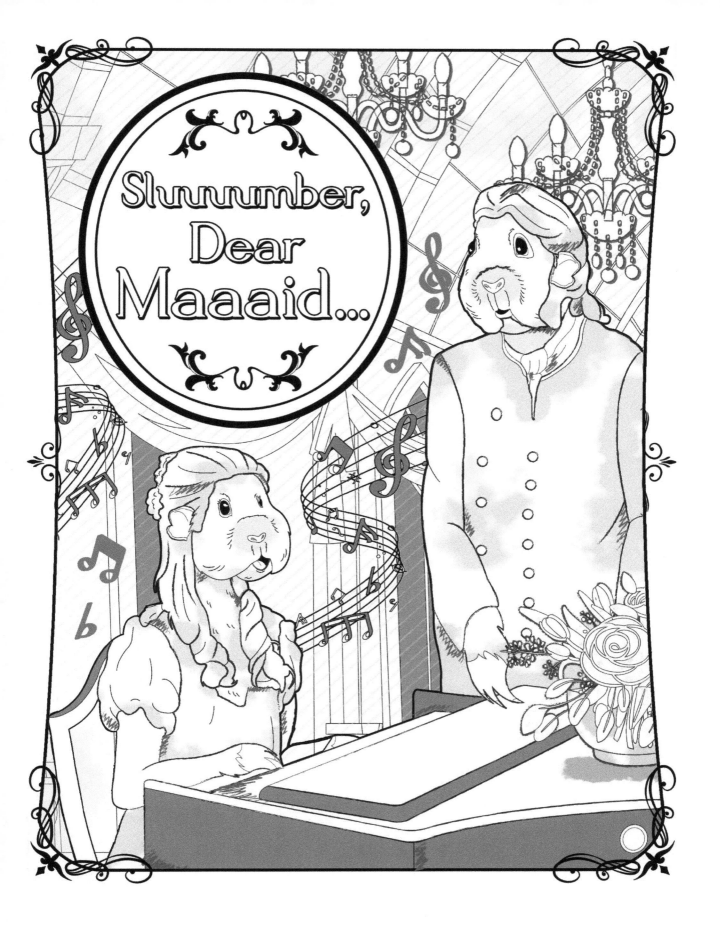

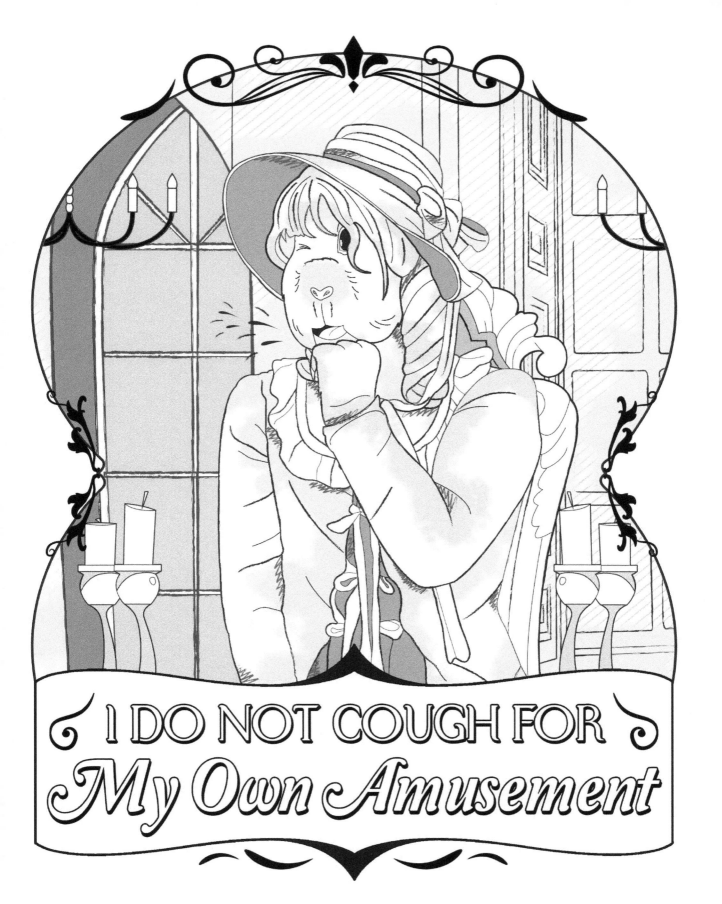

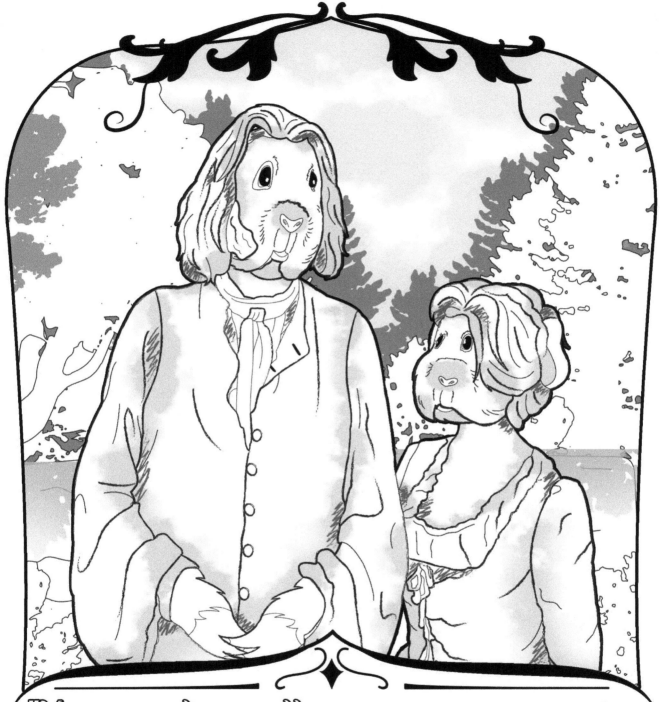

"Your mother will never see you again
if you do not marry Mr. Collins,
and I will never see you again if you do."

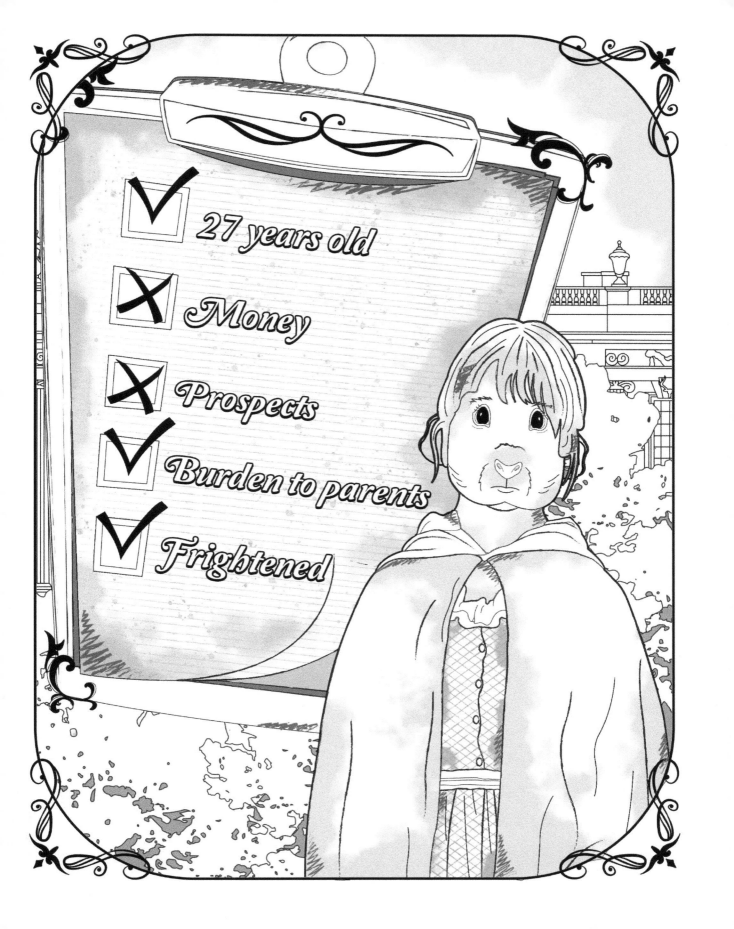

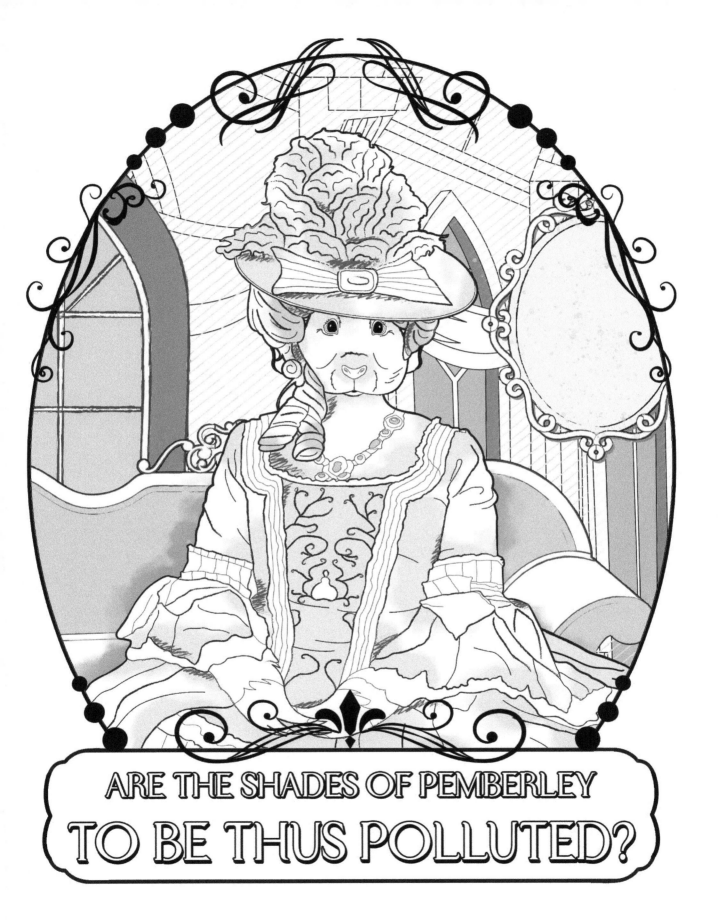

ARE THE SHADES OF PEMBERLEY
TO BE THUS POLLUTED?

YOU MUST ALLOW ME
TO TELL YOU HOW
ARDENTLY I ADMIRE AND LOVE YOU

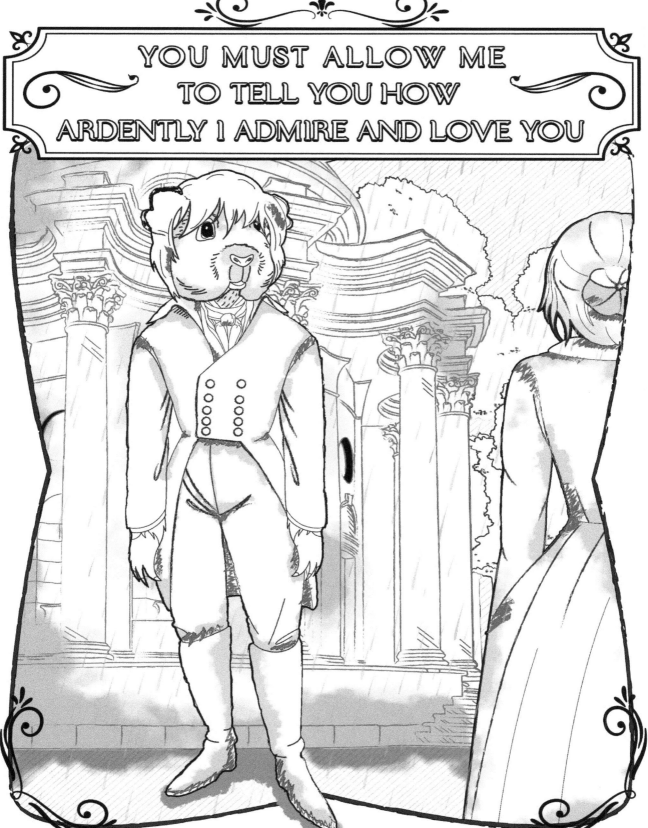

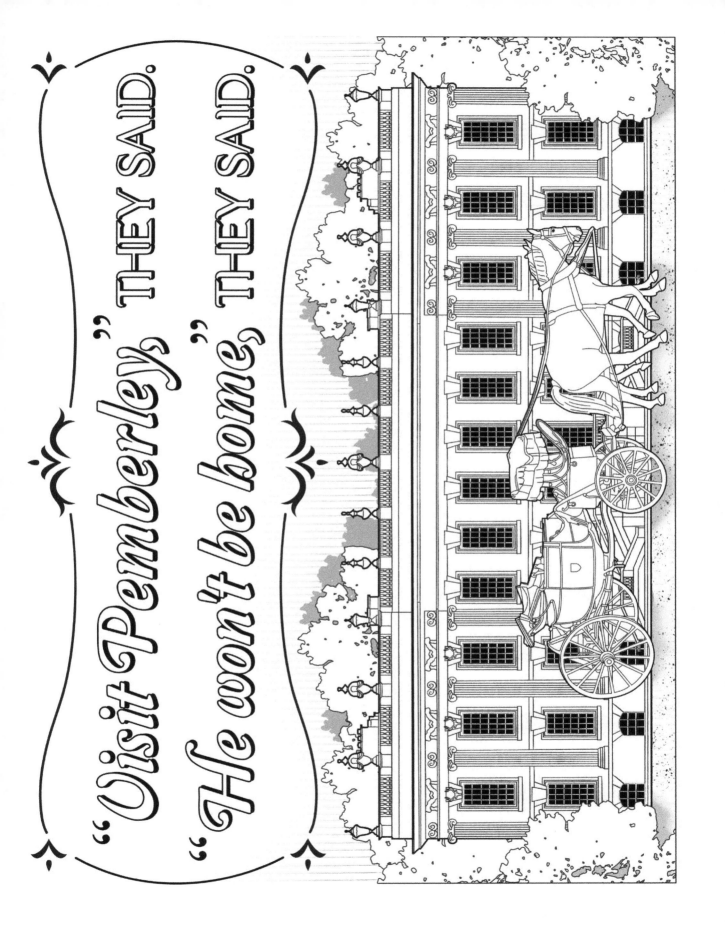

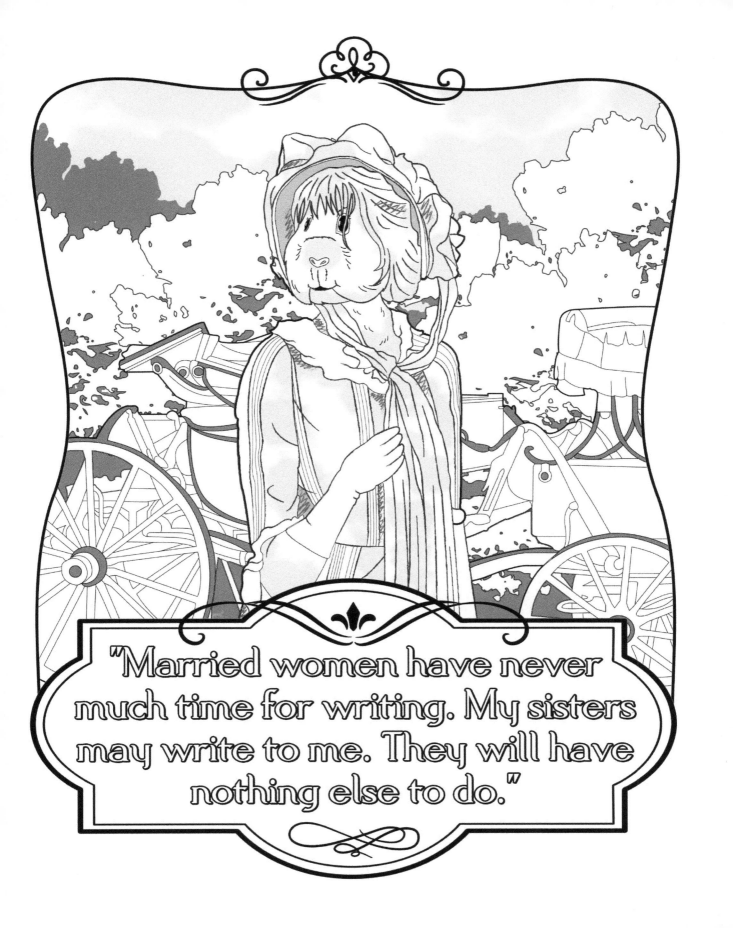

"Married women have never much time for writing. My sisters may write to me. They will have nothing else to do."

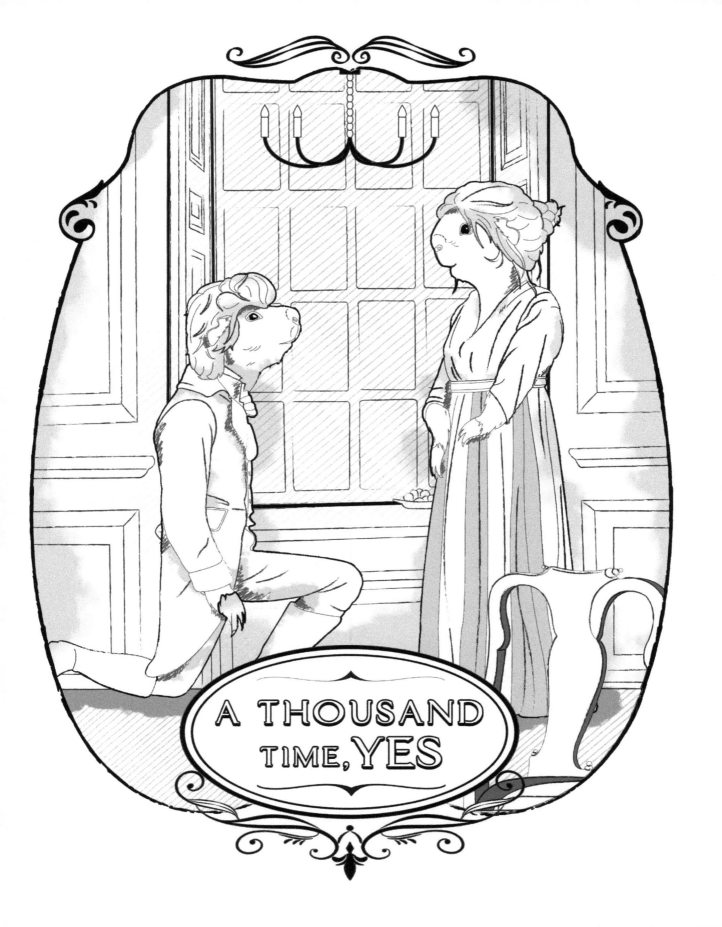

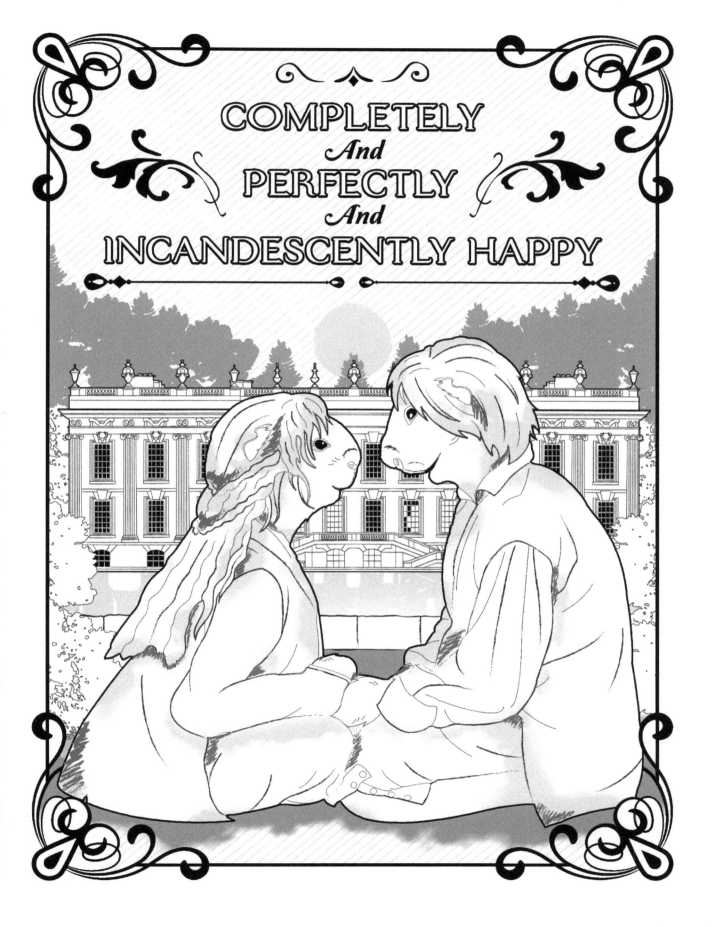

Lightning Source UK Ltd.
Milton Keynes UK
UKHW051943100223
416857UK00015B/160